Collins

easy learning

English

Ages 9–11

poetry

fiction

non-fiction

Shareen Mayers

How to use this book

This book is for parents who want to work with their child at home to support and practise what is happening at school.

Tips

- Your child should work in a quiet, comfortable place, away from distractions.
- Tackle one topic at a time and give your child opportunities to practise.
- Encourage your child to check his/her answers.
- Discuss with your child what he/she has learnt.
- Discuss favourite activities.
- Reward your child with lots of praise and encouragement.

Parents' notes

At the bottom of each page you will find a footnote. **Supporting your child** explains how you can help your child practise the activity. **Taking it further** suggests additional activities and encourages discussion about what your child has learnt.

The vocabulary that your child should know and use by the end of this book includes:

alliteration	bracket	cohesion
dash	metaphor	modal verb
personification	relative pronoun	simile

We hope that you and your child enjoy working through this book.

ACKNOWLEDGEMENTS

The author and publisher are grateful to the copyright holders for permission to use quoted materials and images.

p.25 © Clipart.com; p.29 © 2008 Jupiterimages Corporation; p.42 *A Poem to be Spoken Silently*, © Pie Corbett

Every effort has been made to trace copyright holders and obtain their permission for the use of copyright material. The author and publisher will gladly receive information enabling them to rectify any error or omission in subsequent editions. All facts are correct at time of going to press.

Published by Collins
An imprint of HarperCollins*Publishers*
1 London Bridge Street
London SE1 9GF

© HarperCollins*Publishers* Limited

ISBN 9780007559886

First published 2014

10 9 8 7 6 5 4

British Library Cataloguing in Publication Data.

A CIP record of this book is available from the British Library.

Publishing Manager: Rebecca Skinner
Author: Shareen Mayers
Commissioning and series editor: Charlotte Christensen
Project editor and manager: Tracey Cowell
Cover design: Susi Martin and Paul Oates
Inside concept design: Lodestone Publishing Limited and Paul Oates

Text design and layout: Q2A Media Services Pvt. Ltd
Artwork: Rachel Annie Bridgen, Q2A Media Services
Production: Robert Smith
Printed in Great Britain by Martins the Printers

MIX
Paper from responsible sources
FSC™ C007454

5 EASY WAYS TO ORDER

1. Available from www.collins.co.uk
2. Fax your order to 01484 665736
3. Phone us on 0844 576 8126
4. Email us at education@harpercollins.co.uk
5. Post your order to: Collins Education, FREEPOST RTKB-SGZT-ZYJL, Honley HD9 6QZ

Contents

–ough words

The –ough spelling represents a number of different sounds.

–ough words

- Read the sentence and copy the –ough words under the right headings.

> Although I'm a rough and tough kind of kid, I still thought you'd bought me chocolates that were soft enough all through.

Rhymes with oo

through

Rhymes with aw

thought

bought

Rhymes with oh

Although

Rhymes with uff

Rough

tough

enough

Write your own

- Now write your own sentence using three –ough words from above.

I bought lots of Chocolates.

Most boys in school are rough.

Supporting your child Help your child to understand that **–ough** words may be said in lots of different ways but are spelled using the same letter string (–ough). There are no rules so your child will need to learn **–ough** words.

Word search

● Find the **–ough** words in this word search. Some of the words make a different sound than the –ough words on page 4. Remember to say the words first so you can hear the sound that the letter string –ough makes.

o	c	u	d	c	o	u	g	h	a
u	d	t	r	m	h	b	a	s	b
g	k	f	a	g	t	l	v	u	o
h	n	h	u	j	h	g	x	t	u
t	r	o	e	l	g	w	a	s	g
x	l	u	j	y	u	v	n	u	h
p	r	s	z	y	o	b	q	m	n
w	q	b	h	p	n	z	o	a	s
d	b	o	r	o	u	g	h	h	g
z	c	b	a	t	h	o	u	g	h

ought ✓
though ✓
borough ✓
bough ✓
plough ✓
cough ✓
nought ✓

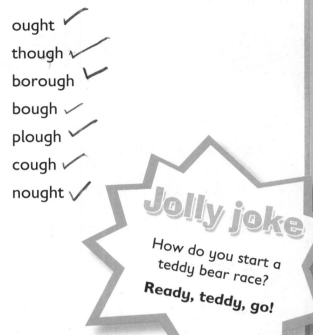

Jolly joke

How do you start a teddy bear race?

Ready, teddy, go!

Write your own

● Write your own sentences using the words below.

● Use a dictionary to check the meanings of the words.

fought	**dough**	**brought**

The 2 Knights fought eachother.

The Pizza Cheifs dough was yammy

My mun brought shopping.

Taking it further Collect five more words with **–ough** spellings and put them under the different pronunciation headings on page 4.

Suffixes

Suffixes are groups of letters added to the ends of words.

Adjectives ending in –able

Listen carefully to the sound of words that end in –able.

- Add the –able suffix to complete the words below.

comfort*able*   fashion*able*   enjoy *able*   valu *able*

- Now finish these sentences with your own words.

My most comfortable clothes are _Jeins_____.

My most fashionable clothes are _Jumpers_____.

My most enjoyable holidays are _Christmas   and   Easter_____

My most valuable possessions are _My tablet._____.

–able and –ably

- Add the –able and –ably suffixes to complete these words.
  Then write out each word in full. The first one has been done for you.

–able	–ably
respect*able* respectable	respect*ably* respectably
applic*able* applicable	applic *ably* applicably
consider *able* consideable	consider *ably* consideably.

Adjectives ending in –ible

Listen carefully to the sound of words that end in –ible.

- Add the –ible suffix to complete the words below. Then cover each word and write it in full.

  poss _ible_   Possible   horr _ible_   horrible

  ed _ible_   edible   sens _ible_   Sensible

- Choose from the words above to fill the spaces.

  If you can do something, it is _Possible_.

  It isn't _Sensible_ to run across the street.

  The ghost gave a _horrible_ scream.

  Chocolate is _edible_ but paper is not.

Aaargh!

–ible and –ibly

- Add the –ible and –ibly suffixes to complete these words.

–ible	–ibly
vis _ible_	vis _ibly_
incred _ible_	incred _ibly_
sens _ible_	sens _ibly_

Jolly joke

What did one ghost say to the other?

Don't spook until you're spooken to!

Write your own

- Write three sentences using the –ible or –ibly words above.

  James Charles is incredible at make-up. ~~Makeup~~

  You have to walk Sensibly down the ball.

  Kelly had to be Sensible in class.

Taking it further Make a list of ten words ending in **–ible** or **–able**. An electronic dictionary may allow you to look up words by their endings.

-cial and -tial words

You normally use the ending **–cial** after a **vowel letter (a, e, i, o, u)** and **–tial** after a **consonant letter**.

Examples:
Spe**cial** – the letter before the **–cial** is a **vowel** (e).
Confiden**tial** – the letter before the **–tial** is a **consonant** (n).

-cial or -tial?

- Complete these words by adding **–cial** or **–tial**.
- Then write each word in full below.

so _Cial_   fa _cial_

Social   _facial_

essen _tial_   par _tial_

essential   _Partial_

Syllables

- Split each word below into syllables and write it in the table.
- Then note down the number of syllables.

  The first one has been done for you.

Word	Syllables	Number of syllables
residential	re-si-den-tial	4
official	Of – fi –cial	3
substantial	Sub– stan–tial	3
artificial	art – ifi –cial	3

Supporting your child Explain to your child that there are some exceptions to the **–cial** and **–tial** rule. Examples include initial, commercial, provincial and financial. Breaking words into syllables will help your child to remember how to spell them. Every syllable must have a vowel but 'y' can act as a vowel sound in words; for example, p**y**ramid, cr**y**ing and part**y**.

Using a dictionary

● Use a dictionary to check the meaning of each word.
  Write the meaning under the word.

residential

residential mean private nursing home.

official

Officail means relating to an alhourity or public body
and its activities.

substantial

Substanial is something large.

artificial

Writing your own

● Now write sentences of your own using these **–cial** and **–tial** words.

official

It was official they were having a boy.

residential

The man ran a residential home

artificial

The peice of art was artifical.

Taking it further   Make sure that your child uses **–cial** and **–tial** words correctly in his/her writing.

Silent letters

Lots of English words have a silent letter. Many silent letters originate from ancient languages.

Circle the silent letter

- Say these words, sounding all the letters. Then circle the letters that are silent.

(k)nee   g(u)ard   (w)rong   (w)reck   (k)hob

Silent letters

The most common silent letters are k, w, h and u.

- List these words under the correct heading.

~~know~~	~~writing~~	buy	~~knock~~	~~wrong~~	build	~~wreck~~	~~knee~~
~~wrist~~	~~honest~~	~~hour~~	guide	~~knit~~	~~wrap~~	~~knife~~	biscuit

Silent k
Know
Knock
Knee
Knit
Knife

Silent w
Writing
Wrong
Wreck
Wrist
Wrap

Silent h
honest
hour

Silent u
buy
build
guide
biscuit

Supporting your child Explain to your child that it might help to pronounce the silent letters in these words, as a fun way of remembering that they are there.

10

wr- words

● Use the words from your silent w list on page 10 to finish this story.

Vic bought his mum a new _Wrist_ watch for her birthday. He spent ages _Writing_ a card to go with the present. Then he got some smart paper to _Wrap_ it up. Somehow it all went _wrong_ and the parcel was a _wreck_ !

Jolly joke

What lies at the bottom of the sea and shivers?

A nervous wreck!

kn- words

● Use the words from your silent k list on page 10 to finish this story.

One day, Bella was in the kitchen cutting some cheese with a _Knife_ when she heard a _Knock_ at the door. She didn't _Know_ who it was, but when she opened the door there was her friend Polly. Polly had brought some wool because Bella was going to _Knit_ some _Knee_ socks.

Taking it further Ask your child to make a list of five more words with silent letters. For example, **lamb** and **doubt** contain a silent **b**. He/she may find it helpful to use a dictionary or the Internet.

Unstressed vowels

In some words the vowel sound is not very clear, or even missed out when the word is said. These sounds are called **unstressed vowels**.

Words within words

Finding words within words can help you to remember words containing unstressed vowel sounds.

a e i o u

ve**get**able – **get** in vegetable

sep**arat**e – **a rat** in separate

business – **a bus in** business

- Can you think of any more words within words? On a separate piece of paper, make a list and practise spelling each word in full.

What is missing?

A vowel sound has been missed out of the following words.

- Put the correct vowel into each word.
- Then write the word in full in the space provided.

int _e_ rest   Interest

freed _o_ m   freedom

parlia _a_ ment   Parliament

carp _e_ t   Carpet

diff _e_ rent   different

fact _o_ ry   factory

comp _a_ ny   company

pois _o_ nous   Poisonous

d _e_ scribe   describe

Circle the letters

- Say the words below out loud slowly.

- Circle the unstressed vowel(s) and then write the word in full. The first one has been done for you.

c e m (e) t (e) r y   <u>cemetery</u>

d (e) f i n (i) t (e) l y   <u>Definitely</u>

m (a) r v e l l (o) (u) s   <u>Marvellous</u>

d (i) c t (i) (o) n (a) r y   <u>Dictionary</u>

s (e) c r (e) t (a) r y   <u>Secretary</u>

Jolly joke

What letter of the alphabet is always waiting?

Q (queue)

Write your own

- Now write a sentence using each of the words below.

- Use a dictionary to check the meanings if you are unsure.

definitely

Mark was definitely going Swimming.

marvellous

Lacey was marvellous at Skateboarding.

dictionary

Sam had to use a dictionary to look up words.

secretary

Mr. Poe had a Secretary.

Taking it further Using mnemonics is another way of remembering how to spell unstressed vowels. For example, the end of the word **would** can be remembered by using the mnemonic 'oh you lucky duck'. Write a mnemonic for the word **secretary**.

Changing words

Prefixes are groups of letters that are added to the beginning of words. They can **change the meaning of verbs and nouns**.

As we have already seen in this book, **suffixes** are groups of letters that can be added to the end of words. They can also **change the meaning of verbs and nouns**.

Adding re- and pre-

Re- often means 'again' or 'back', and pre- means 'before'.

- Add re- to the beginning of these **verbs** and then write each word in full.

  _re_ build   _re – build_   _re–_ place   _re – place_

  _re_ write   _re – write_   _re–_ use   _re – use_

- Add pre- to the beginning of these **verbs** and then write each word in full.

  Pre – pay   _Pre – pay_   _Pre –_ fix   _Pre – fix_

  Pre– cook   _Pre – cook_   _Pre–_ cast   _pre – cast_

Re- or pre-?

- Insert re- or pre- to complete these sentences.

  The audience were watching a _pre_ view of the film.

  As a _re_ caution, I made sure I wore my hat whilst riding my bike.

  Please can I have a _re_ fill of this drink?

  The boy had to _re_ turn to school because he forgot his coat.

Supporting your child   How many other re- and pre- words can your child think of? Try to come up with another ten words.

We can **change some verbs into nouns** by adding a **suffix**.

Nouns can be changed into verbs by adding the following **suffixes**:

–ise   –ify   –en

Verbs to nouns

- Which suffixes can make nouns out of these verbs? Write the correct words in the table. Some verbs will need to change before adding the suffix. (Hint: try saying the words out loud with each ending.)

Verb	–ist	–ism	–ology
hypnotise	hypnotist	hypnotism	hypnotology
tour	tourist	tourism	tourology
cycle			
escape			

Nouns to verbs

- Which suffixes can make verbs out of these nouns? Write the correct words in the table. Some nouns will need to change before adding the suffix. (Hint: try saying the words out loud with each ending.)

Noun	–ise	–ify	–en
terror	terrorise	terroify	terroren
magnet	magnetise	magnetify	magneed
vandal	vandalise	vandalify	vanden
length	lengthise	lengthify	lengthen
fright	~~frightise~~ frightise	frightify	frighteren
material	materialise	materialify	~~materen~~
horror			
light			

Taking it further Play the changing words game on a journey. One person picks a suffix and the other person has to find a word to fit it. Other suffixes you could use are **–ed**, **–ing** and **–er**. How many words can you find for each?

Word order

The word order in longer sentences can be changed to create different effects. For example, putting a character's name at the beginning of a sentence can make him/her stand out and seem more important. Varying the order of sentences can also help to make your writing more interesting.

Word order in a sentence

Look at this sentence: Every day, at half past two, Gill went to the café next to the church for a cup of coffee.

It could be written: Gill went to the café next to the church for a cup of coffee at half past two every day.

- Find at least one more way of writing out the same sentence so that it still makes sense.

_____

_____

_____

Changing the order of a sentence

Look at this sentence: Abdul stopped at the corner after he got off the bus.

It could be written: After he got off the bus, Abdul stopped at the corner.

- Change the order of the sentence below. Use the example above to help you.

  The old lady carried her heavy bag while it was snowing.

_____

_____

Supporting your child   Remind your child that words like **while**, **when** and **after** are conjunctions that add extra information to a sentence. For example, 'after he got off the bus' is a subordinate clause using the conjunction **after**. There is more information about subordinate clauses on pages 24 and 25.

You need to know which words in a sentence are the most important and must be left in.

Most important words

Look at the sentence below. The important words are underlined.

Billy Roberts, the new captain of Newtown Rovers football team, was interviewed in the local newspaper about the thrilling match on Tuesday, when his team won 4—0 in an exciting game against City.

We can take the important words and use them to make a shorter sentence, like this:

Billy Roberts, Newtown Rovers' captain, was interviewed in the local newspaper about Tuesday's match against City, which Rovers won 4—0.

- Now make your own version of this sentence by changing the word order.

_____

_____

_____

Which words can be left out?

- Cross out the unnecessary words in each of the following sentences.
- Then write out the important words in a new, shorter sentence.

  Tall Steven Sutherland, who was 24 in a month's time, had returned from a lovely, long holiday in Australia, where he had stayed for the last six months.

_____

_____

  The guitarist, whose favourite food was broccoli, was playing at his first outdoor concert, even though it was raining, and broke his string in the middle of the first song.

_____

_____

Taking it further   Take a short newspaper article and set your child a target number of words, e.g. 100. Ask him/her to underline or highlight the most important information and rewrite the article in the target number of words or less.

i before e except after c

You need to learn when to use **ie** and **ei** within words.

Most words are spelled with **ie** within them. Example: bel**ie**f

After **c**, you usually use **ei** when it makes the **ee** sound. Example: rec**ei**ve

ie or ei?

- Circle the words that contain **ei** after **c**.

receipt	deceive	chief	perceive
relief	conceit	believe	ceiling

Sorting words

- Now put the words above into the correct part of the table.

ei words after c	ie words

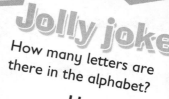

Fill in the gaps

Remember that after c the word must have an ee sound to be spelled ei.

- Write **ei** or **ie** to complete each word.
- Then write each word in full in the space provided.

sh___ld _____   conc___ve _____

ach___ve _____   dec___t _____

sold___r _____   bab___s _____

conc___t _____   p___ce _____

br___f _____

Exceptions to the rule

Jolly joke
How many letters are there in the alphabet?
11
(THEALPHABET)

There are some words that do not follow the i before e except after c, when the sound is ee rule. We just have to learn them.

Examples: **foreign**   **height**   **their**

- Use a dictionary to look up these words and then write their meanings below.

foreign

_____

height

_____

their

_____

Taking it further   Check that your child is using **ie** and **ei** spellings correctly in his/her writing.

Homophones and near homophones

You need to know how to use and spell different **homophones** in your writing. **Homophones** are words that sound the same or similar but have different meanings or spellings.

Stationary means not moving and **stationery** means office equipment like pens and envelopes. The **a** in station**a**ry can help you to remember that it is an **a**djective. The **e** in the noun station**e**ry can help you think of an **e**nvelope.

Whose means belonging to someone and **who's** is a contraction of **who is** or **who has**.

Stationary or stationery?

- Fill the gaps in these sentences with station**a**ry or station**e**ry.

The train was _____ at the platform.

The office had lots of _____.

Do you have a place where I can put my _____ in the classroom?

The man remained _____ while the police officer searched his car.

Whose or who's?

- Fill the gaps in these sentences with **whose** or **who's**.

_____ eaten all of my porridge?

_____ coat is that?

Do you know _____ car that is?

Do you know _____ taking the dog for a walk?

Supporting your child   If these words come up in everyday conversation, ask your child to remind you of the correct way to spell them.

Practise is always a verb and practice is always a noun.
Example: "When I practise my spelling, practice makes perfect."

These words follow the same rule: advise is a verb and advice is a noun.
This time it is easier, as you say the two words as they are spelled.

Practice or practise?

● Fill the gaps in these sentences with practice or practise.

The band has to _____ every day.

I never get enough _____.

I try to _____ swimming every day, but I sometimes

miss my _____ on Sundays.

Jolly joke

What do you get when you put a fish and an elephant together?

Swimming trunks!

Advice or advise?

● Fill the gaps in these sentences with advice or advise.

Could you give me some _____, please?

I _____ you to follow my _____.

How would you _____ me?

Taking it further Practise/practice and **advise/advice** come up a lot: always check to see whether your child has spelled them correctly.

Modal verbs

Modal verbs are used to show how possible something is or was. They can tell you if an action might happen in the future and to what extent.

| might | should | could | will | must | would | can | may |

Examples: I **might** watch the tennis next week.   I **will** visit the library this week.

Finding the modal verb

● Circle the modal verb in each sentence.

I might have been happy with the new rules yesterday but I am not now.

You can leave the room if you wish.

I should have shared my sandwich.

I might have gone to the park but it was pouring with rain.

I will visit the bank tomorrow.

Matching modal verbs

● Draw a line between the start and correct ending for each sentence.

Start

I should have finished my

I should have bought

She would make you a drink

He will make an excellent

Ending

teacher in the future.

a new coat.

homework today!

but she has to leave now.

22

- Finish these sentences with endings that make sense.

I should _____

She would _____

Would you _____

I will _____

He must _____

Jolly joke

Why didn't the skeleton go to the school dance?

He didn't have anybody to take.

Writing your own

- Write your own sentences using each of the modal verbs below.

might	should	will	must

_____

_____

_____

_____

Taking it further   Explain to your child that in addition to showing how possible something is or was, modal verbs have other uses. They can be used to describe a skill ("He can speak three languages"), to give advice ("You must do your homework"), to ask for/give permission ("Could I stay a bit longer, please?") and to describe things we do or did regularly ("When I was on holiday, we would go for a swim every day").

Subordinate clauses

A **main clause** makes sense on its own. A **subordinate clause** adds extra information to a sentence and does not make sense on its own.

Example: My brother, **who is very annoying,** is younger than me.

| Main clause | Subordinate clause – gives extra information about the brother (noun) |

Subordinate clauses can come at the **start**, **middle** or **end** of a sentence. Every clause must have a verb. Remember, **am, are, is, have** and **has** are verbs. The relative pronouns **who** and **which** are used to give extra information about the noun within a sentence. **Who** is used for human subjects and pet animals, and **which** is used for non-human subjects or objects.

Extra information

- Underline the **subordinate clauses** in these sentences. The first one has been done for you.

  I made some dinner <u>because I was starving</u>.

  My pet cat, who is normally friendly, scratched the neighbour's cat.

  Although it was difficult, I still completed my homework.

  The girl, who had scruffy hair, seemed lost.

Subordinate clauses in the middle

- Underline the sentences where the subordinate clause is in the **middle** of the sentence. The first one has been done for you.

  <u>Our teacher, who is normally on time, was late for school today.</u>

  The summer fair was cancelled because it was raining.

  The car, which is old and broken, was taken to the repair shop.

  They completed the run, which seemed to take forever to finish.

  My brother, who lives abroad, is a medical doctor.

Supporting your child To help with your child's understanding, ask him/her to write down an example of a subordinate clause at the start, middle and end of a sentence.

Relative pronouns

- Underline the relative pronouns (**who** or **which**) within the subordinate clauses in the sentences below. The first one has been done for you.

The boy, <u>who</u> was pleased with his performance, scored a goal for his team.

The children, who loved reading, visited the local library.

I visited Athens, which is in sunny Greece.

The children, who are normally well-behaved, started to shout when the teacher left the room.

The shop, which was really busy, had beautiful dresses in the window.

Jolly joke

What is the longest word in the English language?
Smiles (there is a mile between the first letter and the last letter).

Writing subordinate clauses

- Choose the correct subordinate clause and then write out the sentence in full.

Remember to use commas! The first one has been done for you.

~~which was green~~	which was red and shiny
which was huge and scary	who was the best in the country

The frog _____ sat on a large leaf.

The frog, which was green, sat on a large leaf.

The lion _____ roared because he saw a fire in the distance.

_____

The goalkeeper _____ dived to get the goal.

_____

The sports car _____ was parked in the garage.

_____

Taking it further   Explain to your child that subordinate clauses containing relative pronouns such as **who**, **which** or **that** are a special type of subordinate clause called a **relative clause**. The relative pronoun, **that**, can often be taken out of a sentence. For example, "This is the dress that I told you about" could be written as "This is the dress I told you about".

Hyphens, dashes and brackets

Hyphens are little links that stick words together.

Examples: break-in   lay-by   mother-in-law

Dashes look a bit like hyphens, but dashes are used to keep parts of sentences apart. Dashes are longer than hyphens — as you can see! You should not use dashes too often.

Example: I walked through the muddy fields — what a mistake!

Hyphens

- Check all of the words below in the dictionary. Which ones need hyphens?
- Tick the words that need hyphens and rewrite them.

grandmother ☐ _____

headphones ☐ _____

greataunt ☐ _____

takeaway ☐ _____

laidback ☐ _____

carryout ☐ _____

Dashes

- Add dashes to these sentences where they are needed.

  Punctuation can be difficult at least I think so.

  Hyphens and dashes are for different things obviously!

  My joined-up writing is very good or so my teacher says.

Supporting your child   To reinforce your child's understanding of hyphens and dashes, ask him/her to write three sentences using hyphenated words and three sentences using dashes.

Brackets fence off part of a sentence (like this).

Look where the full stop goes!

Brackets

- Rewrite these sentences with brackets instead of commas.

My grandmother remembers the Second World War, 1939–1945.

_____

_____

_____

James, my cousin's father, married June, our neighbour's brother.

_____

_____

_____

Fill the gaps

- Insert hyphens, dashes or brackets in the boxes. You decide!

William Shakespeare ☐ 1564–1616 ☐ was England's greatest poet and

playwright. He was born in Stratford ☐ upon ☐ Avon, the son of a

well ☐ to ☐ do glove ☐ maker ☐ an important man in the town. At 18,

William married a local girl ☐ Anne Hathaway ☐ but soon left Stratford

to seek his fortune in London ☐ England's capital city.

Taking it further Look out for these trickier kinds of punctuation. You will see plenty of dashes in adverts. Brackets can be useful too, as long as you get the punctuation right – usually no punctuation goes inside the brackets.

Acronyms

Acronyms are made up of the initial letters of words.
Example: **CD** stands for **c**ompact **d**isc.

Making acronyms

- Find and write the acronyms for the following phrases/names.

Phrase/Name	Acronym
British Broadcasting Corporation	
Royal Automobile Club	
Amateur Athletics Association	

Common acronyms

- Here are some common acronyms. Look up their meanings in a dictionary and write out the words that make up the acronym.

radar

_____

NASA

_____

RAF

_____

scuba

_____

Supporting your child   Make up some acronyms of your own, e.g. AHM – automatic homework machine! Look for examples of acronyms in newspaper articles or books. Make a list.

Shortening words

Some everyday words are made from longer words by taking off part of the word.

Example: An omnibus is usually known as a bus. The prefix omni–, meaning all, has been missed out.

Taking away parts of words

● Take away parts of the following words to make shorter, everyday words.

telephone _____

aeroplane _____

television _____

submarine _____

Write your own

● Write a sentence for each of the shortened words above.

_____

_____

_____

_____

Taking it further   Ask your child to think of five more examples of shortened words – where part of the word has been removed to make an everyday word.

Cohesion within paragraphs

Cohesion is a difficult word. It means that the writer uses cohesive devices, such as adverbials or conjunctions, to help his/her sentences in a paragraph link together and make sense. Adverbials and conjunctions are sometimes called **connectives**.

Adverbials are words or phrases that tell us about **manner** (how), **time** (when), **place** (where) and **number** (for example, secondly). They help to make your writing flow.

Example: (Firstly,) I would like to thank my mum.

Conjunctions are words that join sentences together or help to add extra information in a sentence. They help writing to flow.

Example: I made sure that I ate my breakfast (because) I had a big day ahead of me.

Adverbials

● Circle the adverbials in these sentences.

Later that day, I visited my friend in hospital.

Last night, I watched television.

Secondly, I am not familiar with that book.

Today, I will do my homework.

Yesterday, the women played netball.

Conjunctions

● Circle the conjunctions used in these sentences.

Although he was late, the boy entered the classroom.

The girl ran home because she was late for her dinner.

My dad tidied the house while I was sleeping.

Everyone watches when he kicks the ball.

Supporting your child   Adverbials are often written at the start of sentences to help sentences in a paragraph link together. However, it is worth reminding your child that an adverbial does not have to be at the beginning of a sentence. For example, "Yesterday, I visited my friends" could be written as "I visited my friends yesterday".

Spot the cohesive devices

- Underline the conjunctions and adverbials used in the following passage. Remember, these cohesive devices help your writing to flow.

Bradley wanted to be a footballer, although he knew it would be difficult. In spite of the training and the early nights, he knew it would be worth it. However, there were a few problems to overcome. Firstly, he had to get over his injury, because he had hurt his ankle in a cup match. Then he had to get a trial with his local team, although he had read in the paper that they were looking for new players. Finally, there was his own lack of confidence. He had to believe in himself.

Jolly joke

What pet makes the loudest noise?

A trum-pet!

Better than 'then'

'Then' is an adverbial of time but it is often overused.

- Add the adverbials to the following passage to help it flow.

At last   A few moments later   Before   Without waiting

Peter was sitting at his computer, playing a racing game.

_____ he could say anything, one of the

cars drove out of the computer screen. Peter couldn't believe his

eyes. _____, another car followed it.

_____, Peter tried to catch the cars as they

raced around his bedroom.

_____, he managed to trap one and pick it up.

To his surprise, the driver spoke to him!

Taking it further   Make up a story by taking turns to think of sentences. Try to use a different conjunction or adverbial in each sentence.

Standard English

It is important to be able to write correct or 'Standard' English.

Agreement of verbs

- The underlined verbs in these sentences aren't quite right. Read the sentences and write them out correctly.

We <u>was given</u> one each.

_____

I <u>drawed</u> a wonderful picture of a horse.

_____

You <u>gived</u> me my present before my birthday.

_____

Correct tenses

The article below should be in the past tense (it happened in the past) but the writer has made some mistakes and used some present tense verbs.

- Underline each incorrect verb and write the correct one above it.

I was walking down Beverley Road and my friend,

Barry, comes up to me and says, "I've lost my dog, Buster."

"I'll help you look for him," I says.

We walked down Olive Gardens and he says, "I bet he's

gone under the fence into the cricket ground!"

We looked through a gap in the fence and there he is, digging up the grass!

I could see a red-faced man who runs up to Buster, waving his arms and shouting.

Buster sees him and got a shock. He tries to squeeze under the fence, but he gets

stuck. Barry was starting to panic, but Buster just got through in time!

Supporting your child Explain to your child that there is a difference between the way we speak to friends and family and the way we write. When we write, we need to use Standard English, so that everyone can understand us.

Double negatives

In a sentence, two negative words cancel out each other.
Example: "I **haven't** done nothing" should be "I **haven't** done anything".

- Rewrite the following sentences correctly.

We didn't go nowhere.

_____

He didn't talk to no-one.

_____

She hadn't not done her homework.

_____

I didn't say nothing.

_____

Jolly joke

What kind of garden does a baker have?

A flour garden!

Putting it all together

- Read this short paragraph and rewrite it in Standard English.

> Me and me friend Judith were on our way to the park, when she says she's lost her money. We looked everywhere, but we couldn't find it. We went on the swings and walked by the duck pond. Judith was really upset and I tries to cheer her up by telling her a joke. We wasn't having a good time, until Judith remembers that she give her money to her mum this morning!

_____

_____

_____

_____

_____

_____

_____

Taking it further   Remind your child to get into the habit of proofreading his/her writing. Apart from checking spellings, he/she should make sure that tenses are correct and that he/she is using the right kinds of verbs.

Dictionary work

You use a **dictionary** to check spellings and meanings of words. A dictionary lists words in alphabetical order. Sometimes you need to look at the first three or four letters of a word to find the word you are looking for.

Alphabetical order

- Put these words into alphabetical order. Remember to look at the first three or four letters within each word if you get stuck.

explanation	exaggerate	environment
especially	existence	embarrass

_____

_____

_____

_____

_____

_____

What do words mean?

- Look up these words in a dictionary and write down their meanings.

exaggerate _____

existence _____

environment _____

Supporting your child   Make sure that your child has a dictionary and thesaurus that is age-appropriate.

Correcting words

- On each line, tick the word that has been spelled correctly.

- Then write the word out again in the space provided.

  Use a dictionary to help you check the spellings, where necessary.

parliament	☐	parliment	☐	_____
necessary	☐	nesessary	☐	_____
nusance	☐	nuisance	☐	_____
opportunity	☐	opportunaty	☐	_____
accomodate	☐	accommodate	☐	_____

Jolly joke

How is an English teacher like a judge?

They both hand out sentences.

Using a thesaurus

You use a thesaurus to help you find words that are similar to one another (e.g. sad, unhappy, miserable). This varies the vocabulary in your writing and makes it more interesting to read.

- Use a thesaurus to find three words that are similar to each word below.

  Write the other words in the space provided.

good _____

happy _____

beautiful _____

scared _____

Taking it further   Encourage your child to use a dictionary and thesaurus when he/she is writing.

35

Legends

Legends are tales about heroes or heroines who mainly lived long ago. They were usually very brave, clever or strong.

A Cornish legend

Read this Cornish legend about Jack the Giant Killer. Then answer the questions.

Jack was a farmer's son who lived near Land's End in the time of King Arthur. The people were being terrorised by a giant called Cormoran, who stole the villagers' cattle. The lord of the manor called a public meeting in the village square and offered a reward for anyone who could slay the fearsome giant. The young boy Jack was the only one who took up the challenge. Everyone laughed because Jack was so small and so young. Undeterred, Jack had a plan. He dug a huge pit near the giant's home on St. Michael's Mount and disguised its opening with twigs and straw. Jack waited till nightfall, then blew his horn as loudly as he could. The angry giant came running out and fell into the pit, where he died.
Everyone celebrated. Jack was given a sword, and a belt embroidered with the words 'Jack the Giant Killer'.

● What qualities do you think Jack had that made him a hero?

_____

● What clues are there to let you know that this story is from a long time ago?

_____

_____

_____

● Look up and write down the meanings of the following words.

manor _____

undeterred _____

nightfall _____

Supporting your child   Discuss with your child the features that are often found in legends, myths and fables. He/she should be able to answer comprehension-style questions about them.

Fables

Fables are stories that have a message, called a 'moral', hidden in the story, e.g. 'pride comes before a fall'. Fables often have animals as the main characters.

Stories with a moral

One famous author of fables was a Greek called Aesop.
Here is a version of his fable 'The Fox and the Crow'.

> There was once a very hungry fox, who saw a black crow with a huge piece of cheese in his beak.
> "Will you share your cheese with me, my friend?" asked the fox.
> The crow didn't answer, but took his cheese and flew up to a high branch of a nearby tree.
> The fox was so hungry and the cheese looked so tasty that the fox thought of a cunning plan.
> "Oh brother crow, how handsome you look up there," he said.
> The crow was pleased with this compliment.
> The fox continued, "And I have heard that you have the most beautiful voice in the forest. Please sing for me."
> The crow was swollen with pride and opened his beak to sing. He let out a terrible croak. As he did so, the cheese fell from his beak and the fox greedily snatched it away and ate it up.
> The crow was left with nothing.

- Can you work out the moral of this fable? Write it down here.

_____

_____

- On a separate piece of paper, try to write your own fable that has the moral '**look before you leap**'. Pick two animals as your main characters and use a similar style to Aesop's fable. Make some notes, then write and illustrate your story.

Taking it further   Read some of Aesop's fables and try to guess each moral. Also look at traditional tales and try to find the moral in them.

Persuasion

You need to know how to use persuasive words and phrases, how to make a persuasive argument and express your own point of view. You also need to be aware of the writer's opinion (**bias**).

Advertisements

- Read the advert below and write down all the examples of persuasive language you can find.

Wonda Pen — The ultimate writing tool!

Have you always wanted neat handwriting?
Have you always wanted a pen that doesn't smudge or leak?
Do you want a pen that can write upside down?
And in water?!

Then you can't afford not to get the fantastic new Wonda Pen!

Impress your teachers
State-of-the-art design
Be the envy of your friends
Perfect handwriting every time!

Have you got yours yet? ONLY £5.99 FROM ALL GOOD STATIONERS.

Examples of persuasive language: _____

_____

_____

_____

_____

Write your own advertisement

- On a separate piece of paper, write your own advert for a fantastic new product that you have invented. Persuade people to buy it using appropriate language.

Use words and expressions like:

Unmissable offer

Exclusive

Supporting your child Look at a range of adverts with your child – on the television, Internet and in newspapers/magazines. Discuss the different techniques that advertisers use to persuade us to buy their products.

Persuasion can also be used in arguments and letters, when someone wants the reader to share his/her point of view.

Using persuasion

- Read the letter below and then answer the questions.

Dear Editor,
   I have been forced to write after reading that the ice rink in Garton is going to be knocked down and replaced by yet another supermarket. Surely this can't be true! Why, it was only in the last Winter Olympics that our own skating star, Callum Richardson, represented his country, narrowly missing out on a bronze medal.
   If the ice rink is demolished, where will our future champions come from? There is already very little for young people to do in Garton, without snatching away one of our best-used facilities. Do you really want the young people of Garton to become unfit or to hang round the streets? We should be building more sports facilities instead of more shops.
   I urge the council to think again. Keep Garton's ice rink!
Yours faithfully,

S Richardson

- What is the point of view of the person who wrote this letter?

_____

_____

- List two arguments (reasons) the writer uses to support his/her point of view.

_____

_____

- In persuasive writing, strong verbs like 'forced', in line 1, are often used. Write down any other strong verbs you can find in the letter.

_____

_____

- On a separate piece of paper, write your own persuasive letter on a subject you feel strongly about. Perhaps there is not enough to do in your local area or dogs are making a mess in your local park.

  Make a list of all the reasons you can think of to support your argument before you start. Remember to use strong verbs.

Taking it further Listen to radio adverts. Make up a radio jingle and record it if possible. Play it back and see how it sounds. Persuasive language needs to have a persuasive voice!

Figurative language and poetic devices

Alliteration is a poetic device but it also helps to make your writing more exciting. Alliteration is when the same sound is repeated in words that are very close or next to each other. It has the effect of making things memorable and ensuring they stand out.

Example: **T**erry's **t**all **t**able

Similes, **metaphors** and **personification** are types of figurative language.

Similes compare one thing with another using the words **as** or **like**.

Example: ... hot **as** the sun.

Alliteration

● Create your own alliterative phrases by adding a word that has the same initial sound as each word below.

seven _____

mischievous _____

serious _____

ten _____

curious _____

Similes

● Underline the sentences that contain similes.

His hand was like steel.

I opened my tired eyes.

She was brave like a lion.

I was as cool as a cucumber.

The slithering snake wrapped itself around a tree.

Supporting your child Encourage your child to use alliteration, similes, metaphors and personification. Explain that using these types of figurative language and poetic devices will make his/her writing more interesting and memorable.

A **metaphor** describes something as if it **is** something else.

Example: ... his **iron** hand.

Personification is used to create images in the reader's mind that helps him/her to understand what the writer means. It describes non-human subjects by giving them human characteristics.

Example: The sea **waved** at the people on the beach.

Metaphors

- Put a tick next to the phrases/sentences that contain metaphors.

Sarah was a brave lion. ☐

Cold like ice ☐

Her eyes were glittering diamonds. ☐

The sun smiled at the people. ☐

His face was an open book. ☐

Personification

- Underline the personification used in this passage.

Steven stepped into a dark and depressed room. The damp cobwebs touched his cold face and he frantically struggled to wipe them away. There was an open window and as the wind howled ferociously outside, the door slammed behind him. Who's there?

- What image does the author's use of figurative language create?

_____

_____

_____

Taking it further   When reading stories or poems, discuss what images figurative language creates in the reader's mind.

Features of poetry

Poets choose their words carefully to express feelings or set moods.

Moods

- Read this poem aloud using expression. Then answer the questions.

> **A Poem to Be Spoken Silently...**
>
> It was so silent that I heard
> my thoughts rustle
> like leaves in a paper bag...
>
> It was so peaceful that I heard
> the trees ease off
> their coats of bark...
>
> It was so still that I heard
> the paving stones groan
> as they muscled for space...
>
> It was so silent that I heard
> a page of this book
> whisper to its neighbour,
> "Look he's peering at us again..."
>
> It was so still that I felt
> a raindrop grin
> as it tickled the window's pane...
>
> It was so calm that I sensed
> a smile crack the face
> of a stranger...
>
> It was so quiet that I heard
> the morning earth roll over
> in its sleep and doze
> for five minutes more...
>
> Pie Corbett

- What kind of mood is the poet trying to create? _____

- Find and copy **two** examples of personification used in this poem.

  _____

  _____

- Find and copy **one** simile used in this poem.

  _____

- Add another verse to the poem, following the style of the poet.

  It was so _____

  _____

  _____

  _____

Supporting your child   There are different types of poems with different feelings. Talk about poems with your child, picking out language and ideas, and saying how they make you both feel.

Some poems tell a story – they are called **narrative poems** and are often quite long.

Narrative poems

Here is part of a narrative poem about a Cup Final football match. Think about the poem and answer the questions below.

In the tunnel
The teams were ready,
The fans were shouting,
The atmosphere heady.
Standing in line,
With racing hearts,
Twenty-two players,
Waiting to start.
The people cheered,
The noise was deafening,
They took up position,
Nerves were lessening.
The whistle blew,
The game began,
The effort incredible
By every man.

Jolly joke

Why are football matches always windy?

Because of all the fans!

- What did you like or dislike about the poem?

_____

_____

- What kind of atmosphere is the poet trying to create?

_____

_____

- Find a phrase in the poem that you like and say why you think it is effective.

_____

_____

- On a separate piece of paper, try writing your own narrative poem. Use something that has happened to you or in your favourite book or film to give you ideas.

Taking it further Read poems by different poets and compare them. Talk about how a poem makes you feel and acknowledge that different people may react differently to the same poem. You could read 'The Highwayman' by Alfred Noyes or any of the 'Revolting Rhymes' by Roald Dahl for more examples of narrative poems.

Play scripts

Every play is written in the form of a **script**, which tells the actors what to say and how to say it. Playwrights use words to show us how a character feels, and directions tell the actors how to say the lines, where to stand and what actions they need to perform.

Scripts

- Read the extract from the play *The Web Monster* and then answer the questions below.

SCENE: **A cave with a huge web suspended from the ceiling. Glenn and Chris, with torches and rucksacks, are exploring. They shine the torch on the web and see a huge spider-like creature with three legs.**

Glenn: (*whispering*) What is it?

Chris: (   ) I... I... don't know!

Glenn: (*dropping his rucksack*) It looks like a giant spider, but it only has three legs!

Chris: Oh... it's looking at us! Run!

Glenn: (   ) No, let's go and talk to it.

Chris: You must be joking! How do you talk to a monster?

Monster: (   ) Excuse me, it's very rude to talk about someone behind their back. The name's Jason, if you don't mind. (*Extends one of his long, red, hairy arms.*) How do you do?

The words in brackets tell the actors how they should say the lines or act.

- Put a word or phrase in each of the empty brackets to suggest how the line should be spoken.

Props are the equipment actors need in order to act out a scene.

- Write down the props needed for the scene above.

_____

_____

The personalities of the characters can be shown in the words they say and the way they say them.

- Think of words to describe the personalities of:

Glenn _____   Chris _____

Monster _____

Supporting your child   Read a play script with your child. Experiment with different voices for the characters.

44

Stories can be written in the form of scripts.

Writing play scripts

Read the story section below. It tells us more about the Web Monster.

In the cave, Jason the Web Monster approached the boys, who were shocked more than scared. Glenn bravely spoke first and asked the monster who he was and how he got there. Chris hid behind Glenn, shaking.

Jason explained that he was staying in the cave until his legs grew back after an accident. Then he hoped to return to his home deep inside the earth. Glenn felt suddenly sorry for Jason and asked if there was anything they could do. Chris opened his rucksack and offered the monster a sandwich. Jason politely refused but asked the boys if they could bring him some milk and a blanket, as the nights were cold in the cave.

- Rewrite the above passage as a play script. Work out the order of the events and what each character might say. Remember to add stage directions to tell the actors how to act and deliver their lines.

SCENE: _____

_____

_____

_____

_____

_____

_____

_____

_____

_____

Taking it further   Go to see a play at your local theatre. Read the programme to find out about the characters and an outline of the plot. Write down and act out your own plays.

Instructions

Instructions need to be clear and easy to follow.

Following instructions

- Read the set of instructions below. Then answer the questions.

Flapjacks

Recipe information
Serves: 8
Preparation time: 10 minutes
Cooking time: 20 minutes

Nutrition
281 calories, 13 g fat (of which saturated fat 6 g), 0.3 g salt, 17 g sugar

Ingredients
100 g unsalted butter
50 g caster sugar
100 g golden syrup
250 g rolled oats
2 teaspoons ground ginger

Method
1 Melt the butter, sugar and syrup together.
2 Stir in the rolled oats and ginger, and press into a shallow 20 cm square, lightly oiled baking tin.
3 Bake for 18–20 minutes at 190°C, 375°F, gas mark 5 until golden brown. The mixture will still be quite soft.
4 Cool for 15 minutes in the tin and cut into squares or rectangles. Lift onto a wire rack to cool completely.

- Why do you think the ingredients have been written before the method?

_____

_____

- Why do you think the writer has used numbers for the instructions? What else could they have used?_____

_____

- The words in red are commands called **imperatives**. They tell us what to do and how to do it. Find and write down four more imperatives in the recipe.

_____

- Why might it be a good idea to use pictures or diagrams in a set of instructions?

_____

Supporting your child Discuss with your child the language used in instructions (commands). Explain the importance of setting out instructions clearly, in the order that things should be done.

- Write your own set of instructions here. Remember that you can use brackets, subordinate clauses and modal verbs to make your writing more interesting.

Here are some ideas to get you started:

how to get to your school from your house; how to juggle; how to play your favourite game; how to make your favourite pudding.

Checklist:

Are my instructions clear?

Have I used commands?

Have I listed all the things I will need?

Have I set out things in the order they need to be done?

- Get someone to follow your instructions to see if they work!

Jolly joke

What do jokes and pencils have in common?

They're no good without a point!

Taking it further   Play the directions game. Direct another person across a room by using clear instructions. Or set a treasure hunt for your friends in your house or garden. Leave clear clues with instructions of where to go to find the next one. Have a small prize at the end!

Answers

–ough words

Rhymes with oo – through
Rhymes with aw – thought, bought
Rhymes with oh – although
Rhymes with uff – rough, tough, enough

Write your own

Check your child's answer.

Word search

o	c	u	d	c	o	u	g	h	a
u	d	t	r	m	h	b	a	s	b
g	k	f	a	g	t	l	v	u	o
h	n	h	u	j	h	g	x	t	u
t	r	o	e	l	g	w	a	s	g
x	l	u	j	y	u	v	n	u	h
p	r	s	z	y	o	b	q	m	n
w	q	b	h	p	n	z	o	a	s
d	b	o	r	o	u	g	h	h	g
z	c	b	a	t	h	o	u	g	h

Write your own

Check your child's answers.

Adjectives ending in –able

comfortable, fashionable, enjoyable, valuable
Check your child's answers.

–able and –ably

applicable, applicably
considerable, considerably

Adjectives ending in –ible

possible, horrible, edible, sensible
possible, sensible/possible, horrible, edible

–ible and –ibly

visible, visibly, incredible, incredibly
sensible, sensibly

Write your own

Check your child's answers.

–cial or –tial?

social, facial, essential, partial

Syllables

of-fi-cial = 3 syllables, sub-stan-tial =
3 syllables, ar-ti-fi-cial = 4 syllables

Using a dictionary

residential – related to where you live,
official – something or someone with
authority, substantial – considerable amount,
artificial – made by humans, not naturally

Writing your own

Check your child's answers.

Circle the silent letter

Circle these letters: k, u, w, w, k

Silent letters

Silent k – know, knock, knee, knit, knife
Silent w – writing, wrong, wreck, wrist, wrap
Silent h – honest, hour
Silent u – buy, build, guide, biscuit

wr– words

wrist, writing, wrap, wrong, wreck

kn– words

knife, knock, know, knit, knee

Words within words

Check your child's answers.

What is missing?

interest, freedom, parliament, carpet, different,
factory, company, poisonous, describe

Circle the letters

definitely, marvellous, dictionary, secretary.

Write your own

Check your child's answers.

Adding re– and pre–

rebuild, replace, rewrite, reuse
prepay, prefix, precook, precast

Re– or pre–?

preview, precaution, refill, return

Verbs to nouns

hypnotist, hypnotism; tourist, tourism; cyclist;
escapist, escapism, escapology

Nouns to verbs

terrorise, terrify; magnetise; vandalise;
lengthen; frighten; materialise; horrify; lighten

Word order in a sentence

Possible answer:
At half past two every day, Gill went to the
café next to the church for a cup of coffee.

Changing the order of a sentence

While it was snowing, the old lady carried
her heavy bag.

Most important words

Check your child's answer.

Which words can be left out?

Check your child has crossed out the
unnecessary words.
Possible shorter sentences:
Steven Sutherland, 23, had returned
from six months' holiday in Australia.
During the first song at his first outdoor
concert, the guitarist's string broke.

ie or ei?

Circle these words: receipt, deceive, perceive,
conceit, ceiling

Sorting words

ei words after c: receipt, deceive, perceive,
conceit, ceiling
ie words: chief, relief, believe

Fill in the gaps

shield, conceive, achieve, deceit, soldier,
babies, conceit, piece, brief

Exceptions to the rule

foreign – from a different country to your own
or something that seems strange
height – how tall you are
their – pronoun meaning belonging to

Stationary or stationery?

stationary, stationery, stationery, stationary

Whose or who's?

Who's, Whose, whose, who's

Practice or practise?

practise, practice, practise, practice

Advice or advise?

advice, advise, advice, advise

Finding the modal verb

Circle these words: might, can, should,
might, will

Matching modal verbs

I should have finished my homework today!
I should have bought a new coat.
She would make you a drink but she has to
leave now.
He will make an excellent teacher in the
future.

Modal verb endings

Check your child's answers.

Writing your own

Possible answers:
I might have been wrong about my friend.
I should have visited the doctor.
I will go out to play today.
I must visit the cinema this weekend.

Extra information

who is normally friendly, Although it was
difficult, who had scruffy hair

Subordinate clauses in the middle

Underline these sentences:
The car, which is old and broken, was taken
to the repair shop.
My brother, who lives abroad, is a medical
doctor.

Relative pronouns

who, which, who, which

Writing subordinate clauses

which was huge and scary, who was the
best in the country, which was red and
shiny

Hyphens

great-aunt, laid-back, carry-out
(These words are correct in the
Collins Dictionary.)